JUST GIVE UP!

When Striving Gives Way to God's Strength

ELIZABETH WILSON

Nova Sei
P R E S S

Just Give Up!

When Striving Gives Way to God's Strength

Published by Nova Sei Press

Tennessee, USA | www.novaseipress.com

Printed in the United States of America

ISBN (Paperback): 979-8-9946788-0-0

ISBN (eBook): 979-8-9946788-1-7

Contents

Dedication

*To **Rachel Hetu**, **Elizabeth Davenport**, and **Kelsi Crew**,
three dear friends who have stayed close, prayed much,
embraced me in valleys, rejoiced with me on mountaintops, and
lovingly compelled me to grow and step into greater.*

*To **Lesley Geers**, a treasured colleague and friend who has set a
consistent, long-term example of faith, diligence, biblical
authority, and being led by the Spirit of God.
For many reasons, I wouldn't be where I am today
without your leadership and kindness.*

*And to **every reader** who wants more of God Himself,
thank you for being here. This book is for you.*

Acknowledgments

This book would not exist without the steady presence and support of those who walked this journey with me.

To my husband, **Dustin Wilson**, thank you for your endless encouragement, patience, and willingness to walk this revelation out with me in real life. From practical help and logistics research to quiet support during moments when the message of this book was still working itself out in me, you have been a constant gift.

To my cover designer, **Jason Gatlin**, thank you for your creativity and professionalism to visually capture the heart of this message. Your patience and precision to apply your talents to the cover of this book, amidst wearing many other hats, is deeply appreciated.

To **Dr. Debbie Rich**, whose life and ministry have impacted me time and time again and who stands as a true testimony of giving up the wrong things to make room for the right ones—thank you. In the months leading up to the writing of this book, as I worked on two of your books, this well-steeped idea was transformed into a written vision.

To my pastors, **Dr. Todd and Katie Holmes**, thank you for your faithful leadership, private counsel, and for cultivating a church environment that emphasizes encountering God, equipping leaders, and expanding the Kingdom. Much of the growth reflected in these pages was nurtured under your care.

To **Drs. Rodney and Adonica Howard-Browne**, thank you for your faithful lives and ministry, which have touched and changed my life from the inside out. Your consistent dedication to pour out the love of God, both on the platform and off, has ministered to my heart for years, resulting in a blessed marriage, a miracle daughter, and a life in pursuit of the call of God. The testimonies and revelation written in these pages are fruit produced from your obedience to the Lord's call on your lives. From the bottom of my heart, thank you.

To the **friends, family members, pastors, leaders, and others** who prayed, encouraged, spoke truth, set a godly example, or offered support along the way—thank you. Your faithfulness, often behind the scenes, made more of a difference than you know.

Above all, I give thanks to **my Heavenly Father, my Savior and Friend**, and **my Helper**. You met me in a hard and weary place and led me into rest, refreshing, and strength that is not my own. This book is ultimately a testimony to Your faithfulness.

Commit your way to the Lord, trust also in Him,
and He shall bring it to pass.

Psalm 37:5 (NKJV)

Finally, my brethren, be strong in the Lord, and in
the power of his might.

Ephesians 6:10

Foreword

Dr. Todd Holmes

It is with immense joy and enthusiasm that I pen this foreword to Elizabeth Wilson's extraordinary work, *Just Give Up! When Striving Gives Way To God's Strength.*

Having known Elizabeth and her precious family for many years, I can affirm that her authenticity, grace, and strong faith radiate through every page of this remarkable book.

In a world that often glorifies relentless striving and achievement, Elizabeth invites us to embark on a refreshing journey of surrender. This book is not merely a collection of insightful thoughts but rather an invitation into a profound relationship with God—one where we discover the incredible freedom and strength that comes when we relinquish control and trust in His divine plan.

Throughout the book, Elizabeth masterfully weaves together personal stories, profound wisdom, and impactful biblical truths. Her notable quotes echo the essence of living authentically by letting go of seeking approval and embracing God's strength. "When you stop dealing in the currency of approval, you're free to start connecting with people genuinely," a powerful sentiment that resonates deeply as we navigate our complex lives. Elizabeth's insight reveals the transformative power of honesty, faithfulness, and obedience, encouraging each of us to allow God to work in our lives in ways we never thought possible.

The chapters, each resounding with clarity and conviction, tackle the heart of striving and its hidden costs. Titles like "Give Up Carrying Tomorrow" and "Give Up the Struggle Bus" are not just catchy phrases; they are calls to action, urging readers to take a moment to breathe, reflect, and ultimately surrender. Elizabeth encourages us to recognize that the delays we perceive in our lives need not define us, but rather, they can serve as the fertile ground for divine inspiration and growth.

As you delve into *Just Give Up!*, expect to find more than just advice; anticipate a heartfelt companion who stands with you in your struggles while guiding you toward the peace and strength found in surrender. This book is an essential read for anyone who has ever felt weighed down by life's pressures or who has battled with the daunting expectations of perfectionism.

Get ready to embark on a journey of liberation—a journey that celebrates the incredible strength we find when we bravely give up all that hinders us, allowing God's strength to shine brightly through our lives. Elizabeth Wilson has crafted a transformative work, and I am confident that you will find deep inspiration within these pages!

With open and eager hearts, let's dive into this life-changing exploration together.

Happy reading!

Dr. Todd Holmes
Senior Pastor of The River of Tri-Cities Church

Introduction

THE INVITATION

This revelation was birthed suddenly from a moment, but this book emerged gently from a season.

As a new mom of a seven-month-old baby, working full-time, just fifteen months after my mom passed, I was trying, I was tired, and I was torn. There was a "Grand Canyon" between the aspirations of where I saw myself and the reality of where I was existing. I blocked God's grace with my effort, and I rejected His guidance for my guessing. I distracted myself with this dream and that activity. I desperately tried to plug holes with my fingers instead of inviting proper repairs. It was chaos I tried to smile through, a mess I tried to tuck away.

But one day, I sat with my journal and wrote my reality:

> *Sometimes giving up is the BEST thing*
> *you can do.*

The light bulb came on, and the specifics flowed like a flood from deep within me through my pen:

Give up doing things in your own strength.

Give up pursuing friendships that aren't happening...and maybe for good reason.

Give up caring what other people think.

Give up losing sleep over the bank account balance.

Give up grieving losses that are holding you back from your wins.

Give up "fake it till you make it" so you can be authentic.

It's always a good idea to give up your seat on the struggle bus!

Just like that, my eyes opened. I saw my seat on the struggle bus, with the cushion deeply sunken from sitting there too long. I finally had a direction, and it wasn't about all the things to fix and to do: time and task management, keeping my stress level down, self-care, or perfect routines for prayer and Bible reading. It was about what not to do, what to let go of, and what to give up entirely.

It took some time for this revelation to supersede my habits, my thoughts, and my "filters." I had to receive healing, expand my capacity, yield to the Lord, and release my expectations. This was a process I began, not a switch I flipped.

Right in the midst of the beginnings of this personal victory, 70% of our combined income vanished. You can imagine the words "just give up" sang out a different tune in my head! We dug our heels in together, determined not to give up our faith or God's promise:

> For I know the thoughts and plans that I have for you, says the Lord, thoughts and plans for welfare and peace and not for evil, to give you hope in your final outcome.
>
> Jeremiah 29:11 (AMPC)

For the next year, we experienced a slew of setbacks. Every time it looked like the big breakthrough, the rug was pulled out from under us. It was wild! As we dug our heels in deeper, the opposition changed from "attack" to "distract." That cost us another six months and nearly took us off course from God's call on our lives. Still, our desperation to step into God's plan for us protected and sustained us.

What must have looked like two people who had no idea what they were doing was really two people stepping into the precise and perfect plan of God. We gave up the wrong attitudes, the wrong motives, the wrong focus, the wrong methods, the wrong thoughts, the wrong plans, and the wrong relationships. Everything we had "tried" so hard to do, we surrendered. And in the crux of the moment when I saw the *real* story arc of the past 18 months—seeing not just opposition but what *God* was doing all along—this book leapt in my heart.

The "Grand Canyon" I saw between my aspirations

and my reality…it was a lie. Where I was existing was on the way to where I was going, not across a great divide. It was a time of figuring things out, not failure. It wasn't a season of setback; it was a setup to step into greater.

For me, the dream and desire for motherhood and children was strong all my life, but as I stepped into it and the pressure came to a boil, what surfaced was the solution for every distraction, discouragement, and discontent: *Just Give Up!*

May this be a strong reminder to stop listening to any lies from the devil—the loud ones, the sneaky ones, the whispered ones, and the striking ones. And may this be a persuasive invitation to search for anything at all within your heart, mind, or life that you must release. This book is about holy surrender, not apathy. It's a call to stop striving in your own strength, not a call to passivity. It's an invitation to trust God with whole processes, not just final outcomes.

I encourage you to let the Lord touch you and speak to you as you read these pages. It's His heart to help you step into greater. It's my heart to give you an avenue through this book to do that, but *He* is the Author and Finisher of your faith. You need to hear from *Him*.

I'm glad you're here. I pray this encourages you to live out of God's strength instead of any striving. You don't have anything to prove—you just have mountains to be emboldened to move.

CHAPTER ONE

When Trying Harder
Stops Helping

WHY PUSHING ISN'T PRODUCING

STRIVING CAN SHOW UP IN DIFFERENT AREAS OF OUR LIVES: mental, social, emotional, spiritual, financial. What probably started out as an honest and well-intentioned goal, and the effort we projected to achieve it, somehow gets out of hand. What once exhilarated us starts to exhaust us.

For me, the person I saw myself becoming was blocked by the life I was actually living. I thought my work would flow better, my day-to-day would involve more routine, and I was well-prepared, with research, intuition, and the Lord's help, to balance new motherhood, full-time work, and my home. I thought our fixer-upper would be finished already and keeping our home tidy and inviting would be simple. I thought longtime family issues would be resolved.

So many expectations I had weren't met. Not even a little bit.

I wasn't so naïve as to think everything would be easy, but I didn't project having to navigate so many challenges and obstacles all at once. What's more, I didn't realize that constantly setting things aside to deal with later meant they were never dealt with at all. Things were piling up. The little foxes really *do* spoil the vines (Song of Solomon 2:15).

As it turned out, the capacity I thought I had, I didn't. And the capacity I needed to have, I hadn't made room for. Things were never going to change or get better on that track, but I kept trying to make all the pieces fit.

Maybe you've heard the saying, "How do you eat an elephant? One bite at a time." Well, I was taking one bite at a time, but I was dealing with multiple elephants. I'd take a bite of this one, then a bite of that one over there, and then notice another one waiting. I was busy but unproductive.

My daily chaos extended into the night, and physical fatigue became an unwelcome obstacle on top of everything else. Rest didn't come easily. My mind stayed active, replaying what wasn't done, what still needed attention, and what I hoped might somehow resolve itself.

Are you thinking I was a poster child for the idea to "just give up" yet? What the Lord wants to do *through* you, He first does *in* you.

In writing this book, I shook my head more than once at my past self and thought, *That girl needs a hug and a heart-to-heart over coffee. Or maybe tea—let's calm her down a little. If she'd just put her eyes on Jesus.*

None of that was sustainable. I had outrageous expectations for myself and nearly every area of my life, without the capacity to step into those aspirations. Worse, I lacked awareness that my own lack of capacity was the real issue. I was spinning my wheels, working hard, and getting nowhere.

When the refreshing wave of "just give up" came over me the day I wrote that journal entry, it didn't come as condemnation. It came as freedom. I was flooded with clarity and specifics—not about everything I needed to *do*, but about what I needed to *release*. Giving up the wrong things would finally make room for the right ones.

This precious key would unlock many doors:

Give up striving.

Living day to day in striving mode feels inconsistent, unreliable, and unsustainable—because it is. There's always more to chase, fix, or prove. If striving doesn't stop, the arriving never happens. You might come to realize the issue isn't "I'm not good enough," but "I'm not doing this well enough."

Some people think small thoughts. We may have big dreams on the inside of us, but maybe our thoughts and imagination work against our dreams. We may hear compliments but not receive or believe them. Small thoughts produce a small life.

Other people are guilty of living small ways. We might think $100 thoughts, but if our actions are penny actions (or should I say nickel actions, since we're not producing pennies anymore?), we'll never see the $100 vision come to pass. No wonder discouragement and disappointment commonly gain such a strong foothold with people. Even the most determined person needs to experience real forward movement at some point.

I was striving in several areas at once, and I couldn't clearly identify it at the time. I just knew I was tired—spiritually, mentally, emotionally, physically, relationally—and something had to change. It was time to pivot, not just toward what I wanted to be, but away from what I didn't want to continue becoming.

The whole chapter of Deuteronomy 28 talks about knowing both where you're called (God's blessing) and what you've been set free from (the curse of the law). In the same way, when you cast a vision for where you're going in life, you also need to take stock of where you are, what keeps you there, and what could hinder you from moving forward.

If striving persists, you don't move the mountain—you circle around it, again and again.

That cycle can end. And it doesn't end by trying harder.

It ends when you finally give up what was never meant to be carried in your own strength.

CHAPTER TWO

The Hidden Cost of Striving

THE PRICE THAT GOES UNNOTICED

STRIVING COMES WITH A COST.

Your body can be exhausted but refuse to settle.

Your mind can be tapped out but won't stop racing.

Something incredible happens, but you can't even locate a remnant of joy to be thankful or excited.

Your fuse is short, and you snap, even when you're fully aware of it happening and you don't want to do that.

You might be needing affection or connection, but you pull away and isolate.

The signs of a coming breaking point are lit up like a Christmas village, but you ignore them all because you refuse to be weak. Your attention span, your marriage, your sleep, your time with the Lord—everything is struggling, and nothing is working. Striving eventually demands much too high a price for anyone.

Diligence and faithfulness are admirable, godly qualities. Yet sometimes, despite the target being diligence, many of us land on "try harder, do more, do better." Or, if the target is faithfulness, we land on "spend more than we ought," whether that be time, money, or capacity. That snare is the compulsion to perform or be approved of. When the pursuit of such pure targets is tainted with striving in our own strength, we miss the mark, because we must rely on God's strength to hit godly targets.

He sets the course, He lights the path, and we are to take the steps in the direction He's given at the pace He's set. He gives us His grace to do what we can't on our own. He gives us His ideas because He's working with the full picture, while we have a narrow viewpoint.

> For My thoughts are not your thoughts, neither are your ways My ways, says the Lord. For as the heavens are higher than the earth, so are My ways higher than your ways and My thoughts than your thoughts.
>
> Isaiah 55:8-9 (AMPC)

When we lose sight of how great our God is, we start living out of our five natural senses, our thoughts (which are unreliable without being renewed by God's Word), and our emotions. We may know the call of God on our lives, and the current assignment He has us in, but if we don't stay plugged in to *Him*, we start trying to carry out His plans our own way. Many of us have experienced this slippery slope at least once. It's a lot of effort with excessive mistakes and inefficiency.

Sometimes we set out to be good stewards of a task. We handle it with care and intention. We seek to honor the Lord and any leaders or other people involved. Before long, though, we pour more time into it. We give ourselves subtasks, and the original task grows and transforms into what we interpret as more significant. Though there's no malicious intent or blatant awareness of an inward shift, we may start to feel important, necessary, as if we're the only solution to the situation. Somewhere along the way, what started out as surrendered stewardship turned into carnal control. What used to be honor toward the Lord and others has now become indifference or negligence.

Striving in our own strength, and not operating out of the Lord's strength, has a way of distorting even what began with pure intentions. If we're striving, we're bringing a performance rather than flowing from and with His presence. When the flesh tries to involve itself with spiritual things, it has a way of making a mess. That's just the reality. As we mix our carnal strength with a spiritual assignment that's pure because it's from God, we end up trekking on an unpaved path we forge ourselves, instead of securely walking on the straight path the Lord prepared for us.

Those of us who have been caught up in striving before know that once we're in that mode, we don't want to stop pushing because we want to be found faithful. But the sad truth and harsh reality is that in the midst of our striving, there's no true faithfulness to be found, only well-intentioned effort at best. We keep trying and growing more tired, having practically nothing to show for all our time and work.

On the other hand, many of us who have been caught up in striving at least a time or two have also experienced the opposite: the peace, freedom, and joy found in yielding to the Lord, fully surrendered to His plan and His way of doing things. Operating in His structure, within His boundaries, comes with a confidence and a security that's unparalleled. There is no place like the secret place, where you have divine blueprints and no missteps—everything flows beautifully like it's orchestrated by the Master, because it is. Why would we want to be anywhere else? Why would we want to do life any other way?

One of the main lessons I've learned in the season of gaining revelation on this "just give up" track is this: If I don't clear out the cobwebs of my bad habits, complaining or criticizing words, and fear-based thoughts, I won't have room for God, His Word, or His will.

> No one can serve two masters; for either he will hate the one and love the other, or he will stand by and be devoted to the one and despise and be against the other. You cannot serve God and mammon (deceitful riches, money, possessions, or whatever is trusted in).
>
> Matthew 6:24 (AMPC)

> And if a house is divided (split into factions and rebelling) against itself, that house will not be able to last.
>
> Mark 3:25 (AMPC)

In the thick of striving and struggling, I couldn't see that holding on to the wrong habits, words, and thoughts made it impossible for me to keep a firm grasp on the

Lord. But I did know that without Him, I couldn't do anything I was setting out to do in pursuit of His call on my life.

I've since come to realize that no amount of praying or biblical confession replaces living a godly life—or makes up the difference for living an ungodly, undisciplined life. I tried to check all the spiritual boxes to have what God planned and desires for me, but I wasn't allowing the Word to transform my character, correct me and reveal necessary changes, and set the godly standard for how I live. This has been a vital breakthrough for me, and the reason is simple: obedience (which flows from relationship) is better than sacrifice (which flows from ritual).

> Samuel said, Has the Lord as great a delight in burnt offerings and sacrifices as in obeying the voice of the Lord? Behold, to obey is better than sacrifice, and to hearken than the fat of rams.
>
> 1 Samuel 15:22 (AMPC)

The ritual of checking spiritual boxes was never going to be the path to what the Lord had for me. Only out of my relationship with Him could I step into His perfect plan. Once I came alive to that word from the Lord—that obedience is better than sacrifice—and realized its application in my daily life, everything began to change.

Everything can change for you, too.

CHAPTER THREE

Give Up Being the Source

FROM SELF-RELIANCE TO SURRENDER

GIVING UP ISN'T ABOUT QUITTING. IT IS ABOUT TAKING ALL the pressure that comes and trusting the Lord to manage that heaviness instead of us trying to process and bear it. We must live wholly surrendered, trusting Him with the tasks, the methods, the details, every area of our lives, and all of ourselves.

Often, what keeps us from surrender isn't conscious, intentional rebellion. It's fear that if we let go, things will fall apart.

This is the essence of our life in relationship with our Heavenly Father: full surrender, genuine pursuit, and exchanging our "too little" for His "more than enough." When we slip into relying on our own strength, we limit what God can do in us, through us, and for us. He wants to bless us with the best, but sometimes we're settling for far below the bare minimum.

If you've ever been invited out to eat but didn't have enough money to eat properly, you might place a "courtesy" order that's cheaper and smaller. It's what you have the ability to pay for. You might explain to your dining companions, "Oh, I just ate," or, "I haven't had much of an appetite today." Little did you know, someone else planned to pay for it. You didn't have to pay the check yourself. You could have eaten a proper meal. You limited yourself and your meal because you didn't know what was available to you.

That's what it looks like to live your life while striving in your own strength: ordering small and cheap, maybe even stressing through the meal, wondering what someone else thinks, or feeling embarrassed. But if you understood you could take your pick from the menu and the check wasn't yours to pay, you would likely feel, carry yourself, and decide differently. There would be a comfortable flow—no explanations, no justifications, none of those emotions or thoughts to manage in the midst of the meal, and no potential stomach growling because your portion wasn't quite enough. With ease, you'd peruse the menu and place your order. You'd simply enjoy your meal when it comes. There would be no tension within you when the check is left on the table.

Trusting God with the outcome doesn't mean disengaging from obedience. It means releasing the pressure of being the source. *God* is our source and supply:

> The young lions do lack, and suffer hunger: but they that seek the Lord shall not want any good thing.

> Psalm 34:10

According as his divine power hath given unto us all things that pertain unto life and godliness, through the knowledge of him that hath called us to glory and virtue:

2 Peter 1:3

The Lord is my strength and my shield; my heart trusted in him, and I am helped: therefore my heart greatly rejoiceth; and with my song will I praise him.

Psalm 28:7

When we are carrying out an assignment from the Lord, the destination, direction, and details ought to come from Him. After all, it's His plan, and He knows and sees much more than we can. If we accept the "what" from Him but then start filling in the blanks we perceive on the "how," we shift from the place of His presence to the stage of our performance. Those are distinctly different from each other. It's as if we tell God, "Okay, I will carry out this assignment You've given me, and I will take care of the details along the way. Don't worry about it. I will figure it out. You can count on me." He knows the end from the beginning! We must stay with Him and make room for Him to help us do what He's asked of us. We need His strength, not our striving.

Maybe for you, striving shows up as staying tense and wavering, even when you know you're doing the right thing. Maybe it looks like over-preparing, over-thinking, or over-explaining. Those are often signs that the load has shifted back onto your shoulders.

Consider Mary and Martha:

Now it happened as they went that He entered a certain village; and a certain woman named Martha welcomed Him into her house. And she had a sister called Mary, who also sat at Jesus' feet and heard His word. But Martha was distracted with much serving, and she approached Him and said, "Lord, do You not care that my sister has left me to serve alone? Therefore tell her to help me." And Jesus answered and said to her, "Martha, Martha, you are worried and troubled about many things. But one thing is needed, and Mary has chosen that good part, which will not be taken away from her."

Luke 10:38-42 (NKJV)

Martha was working hard, and she was agitated that Mary wasn't helping her. Jesus didn't tell Mary to step away from Him and start striving with Martha. Instead, Jesus told Martha that Mary was doing the right thing: keeping her focus on Him, not worrying about anything.

Jesus isn't calling us to passivity or excusing us from diligent work, but He knows we need to take time with Him in order for us to be productive and faithful. He's our source. When we prioritize taking time in His presence, our times of work are faithful diligence, not striving. We are refreshed and infused with His strength.

But they that wait upon the Lord shall renew their strength; they shall mount up with wings as eagles; they shall run, and not be weary; and they shall walk, and not faint.

Isaiah 40:31

God never asks us to do something that we don't need His help to accomplish. He is a God of faith, and we are a people of faith. When striving truly gives way to God's strength, we transition from what was a passive faith (if it was faith at all) into an active faith.

That active faith place is where we are freely accessing blueprints from Him, operating in His grace, and trusting Him with everything. It's the place where we find His joy and peace touching everything concerning us. Surviving becomes thriving. Heaviness dissipates. We lay down every burden and step into His rest. We relinquish all control, and there's an ease to obedience. We see things through His eyes instead of our natural understanding.

If God be for us, who can be against us?

Romans 8:31b

In this place, we are victorious and undefeatable. Faith in God will always win, because God never loses. He never fails or falters. He is perfect in all of His ways, and He sees the end from the beginning. We see right now, we can glimpse some things ahead of us by the Spirit of God, and we can see the past through our rearview mirror. But He sees all of it, all at once, with perfect accuracy. There is no stronger, greater, or safer foundation to build our life upon than God, His Word, and His will.

> Except the Lord build the house, they labour in vain that build it: except the Lord keep the city, the watchman waketh but in vain.
>
> Psalm 127:1

Aren't you thankful we don't have to labor in vain? Today, we can stop trying to be our own source. Today, we can look to God alone as our source.

Declare Psalm 91 (KJV) over yourself and your life:

Because I dwell in the secret place of the most High,
I shall abide under the shadow of the Almighty.
I will say of the Lord,
He is my refuge and my fortress:
my God; in Him will I trust.

Surely He shall deliver me
from the snare of the fowler,
and from the noisome pestilence.
He shall cover me with His feathers,
and under His wings shall I trust:
His truth shall be my shield and buckler.

I shall not be afraid for the terror by night;
nor for the arrow that flieth by day;

nor for the pestilence that walketh in darkness;
nor for the destruction that wasteth at noonday.

A thousand shall fall at my side,
and ten thousand at my right hand;
but it shall not come nigh me.

Only with my eyes shall I behold and see
the reward of the wicked.

Because I have made the Lord, which is my refuge,
even the most High, my habitation;
there shall no evil befall me,
neither shall any plague come nigh my dwelling.

For He shall give His angels charge over me,
to keep me in all my ways.
They shall bear me up in their hands,
lest I dash my foot against a stone.

I shall tread upon the lion and adder:
the young lion and the dragon shall I trample under feet.

Because I have set my love upon Him,
therefore will He deliver me:
He will set me on high, because I have known His Name.

I shall call upon Him, and He will answer me:
He will be with me in trouble;
He will deliver me, and honour me.

With long life will He satisfy me,
and shew me His salvation.

CHAPTER FOUR

Give Up Chasing Approval

FROM VALIDATION TO VALUED

Up to this point, we've looked almost entirely inward. Let's include some external focus now. We're considering the people in our lives, our inner dialogue concerning them, and the relationships we may or may not have with them.

For quite a while, I didn't realize all the energy I was spending just trying to be understood or accepted by other people. Tasks don't typically weigh me down, but I have felt the weight of people's opinions and known disappointment in relationships. Sometimes, a small grief would appear as my desire for certain relationships went unfulfilled. Left unchecked, that small grief would gradually become a large mountain.

This is one *major* reason for God's instruction to guard our heart with all diligence.

Keep thy heart with all diligence; for out of it are the issues of life.

Proverbs 4:23

Do you realize that giving place to a small grief, a mere disappointment, or a slight burden will become a big issue in your heart, such as resentment, criticism, bitterness, unforgiveness, offense, arrogance, pride, or jealousy? That's dangerous and costly in our lives.

I've made the mistake before of identifying with the opinions I *think* other people have of me. And in conversations I've had with other people, I came to the realization that this isn't just a mistake I've made. It's also a trap that other people have found themselves in.

One important distinction we make here is that the opinions we may allow to shape how we look at and think about ourselves are either *assumed* or *known*. If someone comes up to you and tells you point-blank what they think of you, it's generally safe to say you know that's their opinion of you.

What's tricky, though, is the assumed opinions of others. You may gather an assumption from how they look at you or seem to avoid acknowledging you, comparing how they interact with other people and how they interact with you, or noticing something they do or don't say to you. There are any number of reasons why the opinion we assume someone holds is actually wrong. We're different people with different personalities, communication styles, likes and dislikes, capacity, and awareness.

Please don't misunderstand me here, because I'm not making light of the conclusions we draw, whether they're correct or incorrect. They sometimes have an effect on us, which may be quite significant. However, if we want to give up striving and start living out of God's strength, it's important for us to recognize what's happening and why, where we need to make changes, and how to leave this struggle behind and truly move forward without it. This is especially true in relationships.

One of the simplest but most doctrinally sound statements I've heard concerning anger and offense is this: "You may have a reason, but you don't have a right." What someone has said or done may be wrong, but as the old saying goes, "Two wrongs don't make a right." This means we can have every reason for how we feel, but when we belong to Jesus, we no longer have a right to lean into that feeling, give place to it, and allow it to drive our thoughts, words, and actions.

> Or do you not know that your body is the temple of the Holy Spirit who is in you, whom you have from God, and you are not your own? For you were bought at a price; therefore glorify God in your body and in your spirit, which are God's.
>
> 1 Corinthians 6:19–20 (NKJV)

When we allow negative opinions to shape who we are, we start moving and acting in accordance with them. That's particularly harmful if they take us out of obedience to and alignment with God's Word. The Bible talks about counting the cost (Luke 14:27–33). That's so important. When we count the cost of living a holy life, a big part of that is dying to the opinions of other people. The only opinion we can concern ourselves with is God's. We learn exactly what He thinks of us and what our life must look like as we spend time in His Word and see what He says about us.

> For You formed my inward parts; You covered me in my mother's womb. I will praise You, for I am fearfully and wonderfully made; marvelous are Your works, and that my soul knows very well.
>
> Psalm 139:13-14 (NKJV)

> Your eyes saw my unformed substance, and in Your book all the days [of my life] were written before ever they took shape, when as yet there was none of them.
>
> Psalm 139:16 (AMPC)

> For we are His workmanship, created in Christ Jesus for good works, which God prepared beforehand that we should walk in them.
>
> Ephesians 2:10 (NKJV)

> For therein is the righteousness of God revealed from faith to faith: as it is written, The just shall live by faith.
>
> Romans 1:17

He must increase, but I must decrease.

John 3:30

Let the word of Christ dwell in you richly in all wisdom; teaching and admonishing one another in psalms and hymns and spiritual songs, singing with grace in your hearts to the Lord.

Colossians 3:16

And be not conformed to this world: but be ye transformed by the renewing of your mind, that ye may prove what is that good, and acceptable, and perfect, will of God.

Romans 12:2

But the wisdom from above is first of all pure (undefiled); then it is peace-loving, courteous (considerate, gentle). [It is willing to] yield to reason, full of compassion and good fruits; it is wholehearted and straightforward, impartial and unfeigned (free from doubts, wavering, and insincerity).

James 3:17 (AMPC)

Therefore, as the elect of God, holy and beloved, put on tender mercies, kindness, humility, meekness, longsuffering; bearing with one another, and forgiving one another, if anyone has a complaint against another; even as Christ forgave you, so you also must do.

Colossians 3:12-13 (NKJV)

There will be godly leaders in your life, people in positions of authority, who will bring correction to you at times. It could pertain to your attitude, your words, your work, your presentation, or any number of things really. This is important to differentiate from opinions. It's an invitation to grow in the things of God, refine your character, and represent Jesus better.

Obey your spiritual leaders and submit to them [continually recognizing their authority over you], for they are constantly keeping watch over your souls and guarding your spiritual welfare, as men who will have to render an account [of their trust]. [Do your part to] let them do this with gladness and not with sighing and groaning, for that would not be profitable to you [either].

Hebrews 13:17 (AMPC)

One time, I faced a serious battle with offense. The offense presented itself multiple times, and I finally took it, while also trying (striving) not to take it. I wasn't allowing even one bit of God's strength to flow in me. Because it was a level of offense I hadn't encountered before, I let it startle me, and I made a mess trying to process it instead of just taking it to the Lord. I've heard it said many times that God will offend our mind to reveal our heart, and I know it to be true. He seeks to reveal our heart for *our* benefit. He already knows what's in our heart, but many times, we don't.

> O Lord, You have searched me and known me. You know my sitting down and my rising up; You understand my thought afar off. You comprehend my path and my lying down, and are acquainted with all my ways. For there is not a word on my tongue, but behold, O Lord, You know it altogether.
>
> Psalm 139:1-4 (NKJV)

While He cares deeply for us, our tears alone don't move God in our situation, but the cry of our heart moves us toward Him. And as we draw near to Him, He draws near to us (James 4:8). If we're determined to consecrate our will to His, He'll give us fresh grace and wisdom. That offense might not be dealt with outwardly, but the Lord will empower you to overcome it inwardly, and it won't hold you hostage because its power was stripped away.

Offense, while a divisive and destructive tactic of the enemy, presents an opportunity to get a spiritual course correction when we handle it right. We run to the only One who can help us forgive and release, because it's disobedient, costly, and painful not to. A struggle with bitterness, resentment, or worse, hatred, wears on us tremendously. God instructs us to give those things up because He loves us and cares about us, and He doesn't want us held in bondage like that. You may have heard the saying, "Holding onto unforgiveness is like drinking poison and expecting the other person to die." It hurts us, not the other person. It holds us back from what God has for us; it doesn't hold the other person back.

Have you ever met someone and quickly realized you'd like to connect with them? God Himself said it's not good for us to be alone (Genesis 2:18), and He designed us to connect with Him and each other, so that scenario isn't unhealthy. But let's say the person doesn't seem receptive to you or they keep you at arm's length. What do you do with that? You desire the connection, and for whatever reason, they don't seem to feel the same way. How much effort do you invest in establishing that relationship?

We mustn't get a whole complex in that situation. But if we invest too much, it's pretty hard *not* to find ourselves sliding down that slippery slope. We might get caught up trying to change ourselves to become acceptable to them. We might get offended and hurt, and then a person we liked and appreciated is someone we can't stand. We might start comparing ourselves to the people that person seems to like or accept, inviting a little seed of jealousy or resentment. It was so simple and innocent, but now it's a serious mess.

I have been in the situation I'm describing. I have done it wrong, I have done it *really* wrong, and I have also done it well. Here are some things I've learned:

- Some people don't click, and some people that you think you want to connect with are not the right relationships for you to have.
- If you find yourself replaying conversations or interactions in your head, shut it down—

nothing good comes from that. Either the relationship comes together in a healthy way, or not at all.

- When you can pinpoint offense in your heart concerning a relationship that isn't where you want it to be, it's revealing stubborn attachment, and, for your own sake, you have to lean into respectful release.
- Any micromanagement you apply to yourself, motivated by what you think another person would like or accept, you're paying "approval tax" that no one billed you for.
- To truly make room for God and everything He promises to you, you have to pursue Him, not get lost in people's approval, opinions, and preferences.
- You can't love anyone properly without God being first place in your heart. True goodness flows from Him. Kindness and joy flow from Him. Peace, strength, and discernment flow from Him.

When you stop dealing in the currency of approval, you're free to start connecting with people genuinely—no hidden motives, no manipulating others or yourself. The respect and honor you extend to people doesn't come from a private aspiration; it comes from your intimate relationship with God. The right people are attracted to you. You have discernment to identify people you shouldn't be linking up with, and you have the wisdom and grace to handle them respectfully, not critically.

You don't need to gain people's approval, and you don't have to force a connection. When you prize your connection with God above all else, you will find yourself with the relationships He picks out for you. You'll find yourself with divine connections instead of difficult ones.

Today, you can give up relational striving and lay the groundwork for healthy relationships and God-ordained connections.

CHAPTER FIVE

Give Up Carrying Tomorrow

FROM OVERTHINKING TO OBEDIENCE

HAVE YOU EVER LOST SLEEP BECAUSE YOUR THOUGHTS ARE on a loop? Maybe you question if you handled something right, if you shouldn't have said what you said, or if you need to make a change to fix a problem.

I've had nights like that. There have been times my body is exhausted, but my mind is racing. I've turned over to my other side, as if I was pushing the thoughts away, but they were still there. It's like being in your car and shifting in your seat because you don't like what's on the radio and you're trying to tune it out, but you know you need to change the station or turn it off.

When mental chaos is blocking our rest at night, do we realize what's happening during the day? Do we sense the impact of broken, distracted sleep on our daily life?

Sometimes we feel we're managing something well or giving it our very best. We're checking the boxes and there's momentum. We expand beyond what's asked of us, seeking to go the extra mile. We think ahead and we think outside the box, identifying potential obstacles and pitching creative solutions. All of that can be with good intentions and pure motives.

Somewhere along the way, it might become less about the task itself and more about us and our ability to make it happen. We start to drive the bus instead of allowing the Lord to guide the process. It becomes important that our hand is on it, that we decide who is or isn't a part of the process, and that certain people know just how much we're extending ourselves. That's pride, control, and manipulation entering the scene.

Maybe you don't relate to any of that. Yet, you find yourself hyper-aware of other people and what they may think, say, or do. You might concern yourself increasingly with what value you bring to the table, whether from a place of low self-esteem or thinking too highly of yourself. You may check your bank balance incessantly, or avoid it entirely. Or maybe you question what's up ahead and if you're ready for it. Any or all of those things are a clear sign that anxiety, worry, fear, or pride has found an open table in your heart and sat down with plans to stay a while.

Just because such motives are in our heart doesn't mean we're consciously aware of them or intend to operate from them. Still, if we go there, if that's what we're operating from, it's exhausting—spirit, soul, and body. We're in the realm of reason and logistics, and normal, healthy processes are interrupted. Your prayers might get shorter, less frequent, or awkward. Your sleep might suffer. You may find yourself incessantly craving and indulging in certain unhealthy foods, and completely averse to and rejecting healthy foods. That's because whatever issues are in your heart are flowing out to every area of your life.

> Keep your heart with all diligence, for out of it spring the issues of life.
>
> Proverbs 4:23 (NKJV)

> Keep and guard your heart with all vigilance and above all that you guard, for out of it flow the springs of life.
>
> Proverbs 4:23 (AMPC)

It is imperative that we guard our heart. It's vital that we check in with the Lord and ask Him to reveal any impurities and purify our hearts with His refining fire. Otherwise, we end up spinning our wheels, standing still, or getting off track, all while we think we're moving forward and making headway.

We have to give up the illusion of control and break the power of fear in our lives. If we want our faith active and working in our lives, we cannot accommodate fear. Faith and fear don't coexist within us.

We desire directions and blueprints from Heaven, not ideas or methods from our head. If we're faithful with the "what" and allow God to supply the "how," we'll arrive at the destination He planned—and His plans are perfect.

> For my thoughts are not your thoughts, neither are your ways my ways, saith the Lord. For as the heavens are

higher than the earth, so are my ways higher than your ways, and my thoughts than your thoughts.

Isaiah 55:8-9

As for God, his way is perfect: the word of the Lord is tried: he is a buckler to all those that trust in him.

Psalm 18:30

It seems like we forget sometimes that God is actively governing what we simply cannot. He sees the end from the beginning. His heart is toward us. His arm is not short or unable to reach. He is our Helper, our Friend, our Father, our Peace, and our Joy.

With every striving effort we make to stay ahead of our problems, we are sidelining God and taking the reins into our own hands. There's a terrible fatigue that comes from that! We are created to move with His strength and His help.

My help comes from the Lord, Who made heaven and earth.

Psalm 121:2 (NKJV)

God is our refuge and strength, a very present help in trouble.

Psalm 46:1

We weren't built to carry everything, figure everything out, or accomplish everything ourselves. We need Him, and He's eager to help us. Worrying is not preparation, nor is foresight necessarily faith.

Times of instability outwardly don't have to become instability inwardly. In fact, as we stand firm and steadfast in our heart, continually connected to the One who holds all the answers and every solution, the outward circumstances that are so uncertain must bow to the plan and purpose of God.

We must allow the peace of God in our heart to bubble up and come out of our mouth. Whatever is inside something is what comes out when it's squeezed. We must have His Word and His power within us, so that when we are squeezed, God and His Word are what come out of us. We say what He says, we think as He thinks, and we move as He moves.

For in him we live, and move, and have our being;

Acts 17:28a

We are not alone. God's grace is sufficient. Wisdom is putting all our trust in Him, no matter what it looks like around us. When we choose to rest peacefully in the midst of a storm, we're just like Jesus, fearless and faithful.

And there arose a great storm of wind, and the waves beat into the ship, so that it was now full. And he was in the hinder part of the ship, asleep on a pillow: and they awake him, and say unto him, Master, carest thou not that we perish? And he arose, and rebuked the wind, and said unto the sea, Peace, be still. And the wind ceased, and there was a great calm. And he said unto them, Why are ye so fearful? how is it that ye have no faith?

Mark 4:37-40

They that go down to the sea in ships, that do business in great waters; these see the works of the Lord, and his wonders in the deep.

Psalm 107:23-24

Today, you can give up carrying the cares of this life and just give them to the Lord. Today, you can turn your back on fear and trust the Lord afresh with everything.

Fear not, for I am with you; be not dismayed, for I am your God. I will strengthen you, yes, I will help you, I will uphold you with My righteous right hand.

Isaiah 41:10 (NKJV)

Pray this prayer:

Lord, I choose to trust You. I believe Your Word is true, and I trust Your plans for me are good. Your Word says to not worry about tomorrow, so today I surrender my tomorrows, and I lay them before

You. I'm obedient to Your Word as I release all my concerns, and I know You will never fail or forsake me. Because I know You hold tomorrow, I have nothing to fear. Thank You for Your Word, the firm foundation I build my life upon. I love You, Lord. Thank You for being my good Father and my faithful Friend. In Jesus' Name, amen.

CHAPTER SIX

Give Up Harbored Grief

FROM GUARDED TO GROUNDED

Is there anything you're holding onto that you *know* God has called you to release?

When my firstborn daughter was just past the newborn stage, there were times I would look at her and welcome joy, but it was stunted. Initially, as I searched for the reason, it felt far off, fuzzy, out of focus. Eventually, I realized I still had some grief to deal with over the losses of my two babies and my mom.

There are a lot of opinions about grief: how long it should last, how it should look, and whether it's healthy or dangerous. Regardless of any of the specifics, it's best to ensure it's a place you come through, not a place you take up residence in.

After two miscarriages just eight months apart, followed closely by the loss of my mom, I felt like I was losing my dad too, thinking his adoption of me years ago was really tied to the marriage, which is "till death do you part." With tears in my eyes, I asked him. He hugged me and assured me he's still my dad and always will be.

Evidently by that point, loss and grief had become an identity and dwelling place for me, no longer a process to come *through*. When you start seeing additional losses that aren't there at all, you're in trouble. But the Lord can help you if you let Him. He helped me.

God is our refuge and strength, a very present help in trouble.

Psalm 46:1

It's vital to have the Word of God planted and established on the inside of you. If all we allow it to do is dance around our ears, pass through our thoughts, or be filed away in the memory bank of our mind, we miss out on deeper purpose and greater protection found in the Word. Jesus taught that the key to this is the condition of our heart, likening it to soil that the seed of the Word is sown (planted) into:

Listen! Behold, a sower went out to sow. And it happened, as he sowed, that some seed fell by the wayside; and the birds of the air came and devoured it. Some fell on stony ground, where it did not have much earth; and immediately it sprang up because it had no depth of earth. But when the sun was up it was scorched, and because it had no root it withered away. And some seed fell among thorns; and the thorns grew up and choked it, and it yielded no crop. But other seed fell on good ground and yielded a crop that sprang up, increased and produced: some thirtyfold, some sixty, and some a hundred.

The sower sows the word. And these are the ones by the wayside where the word is sown. When they hear, Satan comes immediately and takes away the word that was sown in their hearts. These likewise are the ones sown on stony ground who, when they hear the word, immediately receive it with gladness; and they have no root in themselves, and so endure only for a time. Afterward, when tribulation or persecution arises for the word's sake, immediately they stumble. Now these are the ones sown among thorns; they are the ones who hear the word, and the cares of this world, the deceitfulness of riches, and the desires for other things entering in choke the word, and it becomes unfruitful. But these are the ones sown on good ground, those who hear the word, accept it, and bear fruit: some thirtyfold, some sixty, and some a hundred.

Mark 4:3-8,14-20 (NKJV)

The Bible talks about David encouraging himself in the Lord. If I'd had a true revelation of what that meant in application, I could've had that powerful, compelling, life-giving Word bubble up from within me as I navigated loss and grief. However, I was distracted from pursuing the only One who could heal my heart, and was instead looking to other people. David's situation wasn't vague or minor—it was dire. Look at the context involved when the Bible says that David encouraged himself in the Lord:

And it came to pass, when David and his men were come to Ziklag on the third day, that the Amalekites had invaded the south, and Ziklag, and smitten Ziklag, and burned it with fire; and had taken the women captives, that were therein: they slew not any, either great or small, but carried them away, and went on their way. So David and his men came to the city, and, behold, it was burned with fire; and their wives, and their sons, and their daughters, were taken captives. Then David and the people that were with him lifted up their voice and wept, until they had no more power to weep. And David's two wives were taken captives, Ahinoam the Jezreelitess, and Abigail the wife of Nabal the Carmelite. And David was greatly distressed; for the people spake of stoning him, because the soul of all the people was grieved, every man for his sons and for his daughters: but David encouraged himself in the Lord his God.

1 Samuel 30:1-6

Notice that David and his people wept, probably profusely, considering all the women and children were gone and the city had been burned with fire. The Bible says that David was "greatly distressed" and that the people—in their grief—began to point the finger at him and talked about killing him. This is the context of David encouraging himself in the Lord: facing destruction of property, loss of his family, and death threats from his people.

Grief will lead people to say and do selfish, destructive things. For us, everything hurt...what someone said, what a lot of people didn't say, the distance people kept when most days we desperately needed a hug, and our faith encouraged and stirred. As my husband and I navigated our hurting hearts, we made many decisions out of grief instead of godly direction.

Yet, the Lord didn't come down on David's men with judgment, and He didn't come down on my husband and me with judgment. He never gave up on us. We may have pulled away from Him, but He didn't pull away from us. In fact, He's so good, gracious, and merciful that He was right there waiting for us when we took the first step toward inviting Him back into our decisions and our healing. He's truly so faithful, kind, and patient with His children.

My dad and I made a pact when my mom passed: We agreed we'd cry if we needed to, but we would not stay there through a whole day, an entire night, or days or weeks at a time. We agreed we wouldn't put "death dates" on the calendar—her birthday, their wedding anniversary, the date she died, the celebration of life date, or the date we buried her ashes. We agreed to love and miss her but help each other go *through* the grief process, not spend years in agony or depression, or putting on a brave face despite a broken heart.

This might not sound proper to some people, and it might not work for everyone, but we didn't want to live bound up in longterm grief. We kept our agreement, and the Lord really helped us. When the one-year anniversary of my mom's passing arrived, we didn't know it until several people texted out of the blue to check on us, and then we knew. Even with the realization of the date, we didn't find ourselves in a pit of despair.

Not everyone has a spouse or parent to walk with them through difficult places, but *everyone* has access to the Lord. I'm still standing today, and not because of willpower or keeping up appearances; I'm standing in God's strength.

In seasons like that, the Lord knows what we need, well beyond our understanding. He touched my heart Himself, often using people who barely knew me and maybe only knew of me, as well as a precious few that were close to me. The important thing is for us to receive His healing and comfort, and that involves going *through* a grief process to come out the other side, not getting lost and buried in it.

You may have different situations in your life. Maybe loss isn't even something you can relate to where you're at in life right now. However, many people know some form of grief. Disappointments, setbacks, or betrayal could spark a grief process. Most of us know what it's like for someone to promise something they don't deliver on, and if we don't release them and the unkept promise, we can find ourselves stuck.

One year, someone offered to coordinate a birthday party for me. I was so excited, and I saw it as a harvest on seeds I had sown coordinating birthday parties for others, but the person never did establish a place or a time. I allowed the sting of that disappointment to affect me for a couple weeks, but I should've released it immediately. It hurts us and limits what God can do in us when we won't surrender what doesn't belong to us. I was looking to that person to facilitate my harvest; I had taken my eyes and expectation off the Lord. We don't receive the promises of God from other people. God often uses other people, but it's Him making good on His promises.

Years ago, I witnessed my husband going through a challenging employment season. The hiring process was truly two-sided, as both parties expressed their needs, expectations, and promises. They negotiated an agreement. I watched my husband for many months, as he was faithful to hold up his end of the agreement and extend beyond the original scope as the need arose. However, while the business benefited from his faithfulness, they did not keep their word. That kind of disappointment could have easily become a setback in my husband's heart and life, yet he continued in faithfulness, and the Lord opened a far better door for him.

On the other side of faithfulness, guarding our heart, and keeping our focus on the current assignment the Lord has us in, is always an open door from the Lord to His perfect will and plan for us.

Besides grief or loss, there are several other things you might be holding onto that God has asked you to release. What about old habits? An old way of thinking about yourself? The Lord has the way through for you, and He will help you.

> Behold, I will do a new thing; now it shall spring forth; shall ye not know it? I will even make a way in the wilderness, and rivers in the desert.
>
> Isaiah 43:19

Certain things don't belong to us because we belong to God. The best way to ensure we release what doesn't belong to us is to spend time with Him, invite Him to speak to and help us, and let Him flow through the vulnerable or hardened places in our heart with His rivers of living water. The most peaceful place is in His presence. The purest love comes from Him.

There is no fear in love; but perfect love casts out fear,

1 John 4:18a (NKJV)

Is there anything you're holding onto that God has called you to release? Would you run to Him and release it now? You may have to release it again in a few hours or tomorrow, but if you are persistent to give it to the Lord each time it comes knocking, you'll find He's carrying it for you. As you make room for more of Him in your heart and life, He's giving you *all* of what He has.

To appoint unto them that mourn in Zion, to give unto them beauty for ashes, the oil of joy for mourning, the garment of praise for the spirit of heaviness; that they might be called trees of righteousness, the planting of the Lord, that he might be glorified.

Isaiah 61:3

He offers you a divine exchange today. There's no burden you're carrying that you can't lay down before Him; He will take it all for you. He loves you so much. He wants to help you, and He offers you His rest, not just for a moment but throughout your daily life.

> Come unto me, all ye that labour and are heavy laden, and I will give you rest. Take my yoke upon you, and learn of me; for I am meek and lowly in heart: and ye shall find rest unto your souls. For my yoke is easy, and my burden is light.
>
> Matthew 11:28-30

Let's highlight some of God's promises together, ones that speak to specific situations. These may not all be the prescription your heart is crying out for right now, but they are all worthy of being planted in your heart because they are God's promises. Should you need them for yourself or someone else, once they're in you, they can come out of you to bring the help and healing needed.

- Death of someone you knew, loved, connected with, or admired: **Psalm 121:1–2** — I will lift up mine eyes unto the hills, from whence cometh my help. My help cometh from the Lord, which made heaven and earth.
- Betrayal of trust or relationship: **Psalm 147:3** — He healeth the broken in heart, and bindeth up their wounds.
- Seeing yourself in a negative, unworthy, or incapable manner: **Romans 8:1** — There is therefore now no condemnation to them which

are in Christ Jesus, who walk not after the flesh, but after the Spirit.

- Identifying with others' opinions, statements, or judgments of you: **1 Peter 2:9 (NKJV)** — But you are a chosen generation, a royal priesthood, a holy nation, His own special people, that you may proclaim the praises of Him who called you out of darkness into His marvelous light.

- Closed door that you don't understand or agree with: **Romans 8:28** — And we know that all things work together for good to them that love God, to them who are the called according to his purpose.

- Estranged family relationships: **Malachi 4:6a (AMPC)** — And he shall turn and reconcile the hearts of the [estranged] fathers to the [ungodly] children, and the hearts of the [rebellious] children to [the piety of] their fathers [a reconciliation produced by repentance of the ungodly].

- Investing deeply in someone who did not seem to reciprocate or appreciate: **Galatians 6:9** — And let us not be weary in well doing: for in due season we shall reap, if we faint not.

- Feeling forgotten, overlooked, or replaced: **Luke 12:6–7 (NKJV)** — Are not five sparrows sold for two copper coins? And not one of them is forgotten before God. But the very hairs of your head are all numbered. Do not fear therefore; you are of more value than many sparrows.

- Measuring yourself by comparison instead of calling: **Galatians 6:4 (AMPC)** — But let every person carefully scrutinize and examine and test his own conduct and his own work. He can then have the personal satisfaction and joy of doing something commendable [in itself alone] without [resorting to] boastful comparison with his neighbor.
- A promise that seems stalled or absent: **Jeremiah 17:7–8 (NKJV)** — Blessed is the man who trusts in the Lord, and whose hope is the Lord. For he shall be like a tree planted by the waters, which spreads out its roots by the river, and will not fear when heat comes; but its leaf will be green, and will not be anxious in the year of drought, nor will cease from yielding fruit.
- Fear of hoping again after disappointment: **Psalm 34:4 (AMPC)** — I sought (inquired of) the Lord and required Him [of necessity and on the authority of His Word], and He heard me, and delivered me from all my fears.
- Feeling like you missed God's timing: **Habakkuk 2:3 (NKJV)** — For the vision is yet for an appointed time; but at the end it will speak, and it will not lie. Though it tarries, wait for it; because it will surely come, it will not tarry.
- Seeing others receive what you're still believing for: **Romans 2:11** — For there is no respect of persons with God.

Make it a habit to search for scriptures that address your situation. This shifts the focus off the problem and onto the solution. We may have questions and feel like others cannot understand, but the devil uses the same tactics and tells the same lies, and God's truth reigns supreme. When we take His Word and apply it to our situations, confessing it from our mouth and letting it minister to our heart, we're making the decision to not succumb to circumstance, but to turn the tide of that circumstance with the help of the Almighty. There are significant trials and temptations we encounter in our lives, but we must let God's Word have the final say.

> I have told you these things, so that in Me you may have [perfect] peace and confidence. In the world you have tribulation and trials and distress and frustration; but be of good cheer [take courage; be confident, certain, undaunted]! For I have overcome the world. [I have deprived it of power to harm you and have conquered it for you.]
>
> John 16:33 (AMPC)

Today, you can release what doesn't belong to you. It doesn't mean things didn't happen, but it does mean those things don't continue to weigh you down, cause you pain or suffering, or block you from receiving His joy, His peace, His strength.

Today, you can be restored. Today, you can be refreshed and revived.

CHAPTER SEVEN

Give Up Polished Presentation

FROM PERFORMANCE TO PRESENCE

Performance says, "I've got this." Faith says, "God's got this." When we stop trying to *look* strong on our own, we allow God to *be* strong through us.

Some people equate discipline with performance, but healthy spiritual discipline is no performance. While both can look like effort producing a positive outcome, the heart behind discipline is godly, and the heart behind performance is not. Discipline flows from an intimate relationship with God, while performance works for approval or image.

You've probably heard the saying, "Fake it till you make it." While it's often said in a playful manner among coworkers or friends, it isn't kind or honest to fake something. For many people, the saying is synonymous with keeping a good attitude or not throwing in the towel while we're figuring out what we're doing. Think about this phrase for a moment, though. Isn't it a method in which you present yourself differently from who, how, and where you truly are?

Such performance is costly, increasingly so. Keeping up appearances means focus is on impression rather than intimacy. God wants our heart, our relationship, our honesty, and our authenticity. David is dubbed "a man after God's own heart." When you read his psalms, don't you think some of his approaches to the Lord involved a serious "ugly cry" at times? When the prophet Nathan called him out on his sins of adultery and murder, do you notice the switch David flips, crying out to God in heartfelt repentance, promptly pursuing forgiveness and persistently petitioning for the child to live? That flipped switch was David shifting back to authenticity, quickly. That's a heart after God's heart.

In contrast, look at Ananias and Sapphira in Acts 5:1–11. They conspired together to lie about the offering they were giving. Worse than that, they weren't just trying to pull one over on the apostles but on God Himself. Talk about a performance! The cost was both their lives.

Additionally, we can see Judas Iscariot putting on a show in John 12:1–6. He declared it was a total waste for Mary to anoint Jesus' feet with precious and costly perfume, suggesting it should have been sold instead so the money could be given to the poor. In reality, his heart was hardened and filled with greed, and he was completely oblivious to Mary's act of love and worship toward Jesus. His outward concern was really inward corruption. The immediate cost was further hardening of his heart, and when you keep reading, you see that the ultimate cost was his life.

And not a creature exists that is concealed from His sight, but all things are open and exposed, naked and defenseless to the eyes of Him with Whom we have to do.

Hebrews 4:13 (AMPC)

God sees and knows everything. There is nothing hidden from Him. The cost of performance is not a price we want to pay. It's exasperating and consuming—physically, mentally, emotionally, and spiritually. Think of it like the growing destruction of a black hole: the more it pulls in, the more strength it has to pull more in. The more we operate in destructive performance, the more destructive performance we're inclined to operate in.

Authenticity has a cost as well, and it's a holy and precious one to pay because when we do, we have full access to Almighty God, our Heavenly Father. It's the same cost that Jesus compelled us to count. The things of God are connected, not bullet points to be cherry-picked. There's always more to discover in His Word and more to experience in His presence.

If we truly belong to Jesus and abide in Him, we'll be like Him, and we'll allow Him to be not just the Savior of our soul but the Lord of our life.

Abide in Me, and I in you. As the branch cannot bear fruit of itself, unless it abides in the vine, neither can you, unless you abide in Me.

If you abide in Me, and My words abide in you, you will ask what you desire, and it shall be done for you. By this My Father is glorified, that you bear much fruit; so you will be My disciples.

John 15:4,7-8 (NKJV)

This costs *everything*. We lay down pride, and we grow in humility. We silence distractions and listen for directions. We give up anxiety and worry, instead being consumed with peace and joy from Heaven. We don't sacrifice our commitment to the Lord to maintain an esteemed reputation among men. We do not compromise our faith to accommodate today's culture. We do things differently. We pursue holiness, not accolades. We care what God thinks, not people and not ourselves. The intimacy with God that we gain is worth any price we could pay.

To be honest, to fully trust in God, is to surrender *all* to Him. This isn't weakness; it's obedience, honor, love. There are many times it might seem easier or more convenient to lie or present yourself in a manner inconsistent with what's truly in your heart, but that price is costly to pay and a great risk. Jesus said in Matthew 7:21–23 that people will stand before Him, expecting to enter Heaven after a life of prophesying in His Name and performing miracles, but He will say, "Depart from Me, you worker of iniquity. I never knew you." The ultimate performers will not enter Heaven at the end of their life. That is a sobering realization.

God's strength can only flow into the areas of your life where you are being honest, faithful, and obedient. No performance we set out to broadcast in our own ability will leave room for God to move, speak, or accomplish His will in our lives. Jesus rebuked such performance, particularly among the religious leaders:

> Then Jesus said to the multitudes and to His disciples, The scribes and Pharisees sit on Moses' seat [of authority]. So observe and practice all they tell you; but do not do what they do, for they preach, but do not practice. They tie up heavy loads, hard to bear, and place them on men's shoulders, but they themselves will not lift a finger to help bear them. They do all their works to be seen of men; for they make wide their phylacteries (small cases enclosing certain Scripture passages, worn during prayer on the left arm and forehead) and make long their fringes [worn by all male Israelites, according to the command]. And they take pleasure in and [thus] love the place of honor at feasts and the best seats in the synagogues, and to be greeted with honor in the marketplaces and to have people call them rabbi.
>
> Matthew 23:1-7 (AMPC)

Notice how Jesus started this teaching with honoring leadership and authority, obeying the Word of God they teach from in their instruction to us. But He also says we are not to do what they do if it's not lining up with God's Word. We follow others as they follow Christ, the Word (1 Corinthians 11:1).

In 1 Kings 18, we can read about the prophet Obadiah, who was a godly man serving the ungodly King Ahab, which made him privy to inside information. Obadiah's faithfulness to God and respect for Ahab's position of authority made room for him to be mightily used of God, saving the lives of hundreds of God's prophets. So, respecting positions of authority (which is obedience to God) can be the difference between being used by God or not. Performance doesn't open those kinds of doors, because it doesn't impress or honor God.

Performance can show up in our workplace, in our home, in our routine errands, in our church, in our relationship with the Lord, anywhere at all. If we're not continually and intentionally honest and abiding in the Lord, it's possible we may fall into the pit of performance somewhere in our lives. Once it's present in one area, it can seep into other areas. The religious leaders that Jesus rebuked for their performance could have chosen to repent and humble themselves before God, but performance had become their perceived righteousness, and humility was far from them. We see a stubbornness in them throughout the four gospels, as they responded with anger and attempts to take Jesus out.

Some people cannot find it in themselves to rejoice with others because they are caught up in their own performance.

Every way of a man is right in his own eyes: but the Lord pondereth the hearts.

Proverbs 21:2

Unto the pure all things are pure: but unto them that are

defiled and unbelieving is nothing pure; but even their mind and conscience is defiled.

Titus 1:15

You can share incredible testimonies of the Lord moving in your life, but performing people can't even find a "Praise God!" to utter in response. You might achieve something incredible and be eager to share with them, only to be met with a brushing past of your news as they declare the mundane happenings of their own life.

Understand, when others are performing, they don't have the capacity to recognize your faithfulness. When others are caught up in their own plans, even if they say they're God's plans, they don't perceive the magnitude of your obedience and rejoice in your accomplishment. Pray for people who are performing. Realize that performance is rooted in fear, and realize that God's perfect love casts out fear. So, just love them with the love of God in your speech, actions, and prayers. Intentionally remember them in your prayers. God's plan is for them to break free.

Anywhere you invite Him to correct you, He will, because He loves and desires the best for you. Ask the Lord to help you recognize if you're ever dismissive of someone else's faithfulness, obedience, or rejoicing in the plans of God coming to pass in their life. Choose to be an encouragement, not a stumbling block.

Rejoice with them that do rejoice,

Romans 12:15a

Do not despise these small beginnings, for the Lord rejoices to see the work begin,

Zechariah 4:10a (NLT)

My mom is in Heaven today, but when she was on this Earth, just about anyone who knew her would say that she connected people, celebrated people, and cared deeply about people. As her daughter, sometimes in my early adulthood I misread her discipleship of others as disregard for me. But she was about her Father's business, ministering the love of God to people that others had written off and considered more effort or time than they were willing to offer. She saw people in the middle of their mess as precious, destined for great things that the Lord planned for them. I'm so thankful she moved with God's heart toward other people; that's an example I witnessed up close, and I saw the good fruit produced in those people's lives. In a short time, I saw their small beginnings grow because my mom was persistent to sow the Word, demonstrate the love of God, and pray over those people. She left the ninety-nine for the one, and she brought the Kingdom of Heaven to their lives, doorsteps, and hearts.

What man of you, having a hundred sheep, if he loses one of them, does not leave the ninety-nine in the wilderness, and go after the one which is lost until he finds it? And when he has found it, he lays it on his shoulders, rejoicing. And when he comes home, he calls together his friends and neighbors, saying to them,

"Rejoice with me, for I have found my sheep which was lost!" I say to you that likewise there will be more joy in heaven over one sinner who repents than over ninety-nine just persons who need no repentance.

Luke 15:4-7 (NKJV)

And from the days of John the Baptist until now the kingdom of heaven suffers violence, and the violent take it by force.

Matthew 11:12 (NKJV)

We must be persistent and driven to distribute the love of God to people. This isn't a striving effort of ourselves; it's a pouring out of God Himself. There's no performance in the presence of God. It's His promises lighting up in people's hearts. It's His kindness and compassion reaching out to brokenness and making it whole. It's the dead dreams being resurrected to new life for God's glory. It's not about us, so it can't be a performance. It's all about Him and the love He has for His most prized and precious creation: people.

Like most couples, my husband and I have had disagreements we've had to resolve over the course of our years together. I tend to have a "present moment" focus initially and am inclined to further depth or implications later, but right out the gate my husband appreciates identification of the "root issue." Over time, we've learned to work with each other fairly well regardless of that core communication difference, because there's authenticity and honesty keeping us connected.

When people have a conflict or disagreement to resolve, there are two routes for each person to take: fake or authentic. If both truly desire to resolve the issue, any differences they have won't stop them. If one or both only want to "win," be considered right, or gain superiority over the other, it's fake, disingenuous, arrogant, and dishonest.

God's strength can flow into your conflict resolution when your words are honest and your heart has pure motives. One caveat: those "pure motives" are only pure if they're godly and biblical, not mere good intentions.

My husband and I have had business dealings with other people where we meant well, but the motive of our heart was to exceed the expectations of the other people involved. We wanted to bless them...and impress them. Does that sound muddy to you? Every time, it was a mess. If our motive had been pure, focused on honesty and counting the full cost of what was involved, we could've projected accurate deadlines and *truly* blessed the people involved. Instead, we presented a stumbling block in their lives with the business deal and in each other's lives at home.

Our *fake* strength blocks God's *real* strength from flowing. In our daily lives, we have many choices to either perform from our efforts or move in total trust and obedience to God. One word of His wisdom in your ear can change the entire trajectory of your life. When He speaks, do you hear Him? If you hear Him, do you trust

Him? If you trust Him, do you obey? Freedom begins where pretending ends.

Is it possible for you to be *more* authentic with the Lord?

Is it possible for you to be *more* authentic with other people?

Is it possible for you to be *more* authentic with yourself?

Today, you can leave any impure motive or fake approach behind. Invite God to help you and correct you. He will never leave you hanging. He will always come through for you where you make room for Him to move.

Declare this:

I humble myself today, and God Himself will exalt me. I refuse to be lifted up in pride, manipulate situations, or live any kind of lie before God, myself, or people. I don't have to try to impress anyone. I live my life to honor God. He's the strength of my life and the restorer of my soul. I choose authenticity, which is me being more like my Father God, who does not and cannot lie. I'm honest, I have pure motives, and I receive correction when it comes. I live my life with clean hands and a pure heart.

CHAPTER EIGHT

Give Up Your Timeline

FROM PRESSURE TO PROCESS

SOMETIMES THE HARDEST THINGS TO SURRENDER AREN'T sins or struggles. They're expectations.

Have you ever felt "behind" in your life? I'm not talking about simple things in your daily life, like consistently doing four laundry loads a week or meal prepping every Monday. I'm talking about the big picture: your greatest dreams, goals, and aspirations. Have you ever considered where you are and found it's not where you wanted to be by now? Disappointment or discouragement might slip in there.

Maybe, like me, you've at least once looked at someone else who got started later than you but seems to be going farther than you already. Comparison like that creeps up on a lot of people every day. What about the deadlines you create or decide on, but you just can't seem to meet them? Frustration with yourself and condemnation could find an open door and walk right in.

Bold and confident trust in God is diminished when

we do not surrender our expectations to Him. He needs our all so He can give us His all.

> Come to Me, all you who labor and are heavy laden, and I will give you rest. Take My yoke upon you and learn from Me, for I am gentle and lowly in heart, and you will find rest for your souls. For My yoke is easy and My burden is light.
>
> Matthew 11:28–30 (NKJV)

This alternate translation of verse 28 conveys the promise in greater detail:

> Come to Me, all you who labor and are heavy-laden and overburdened, and I will cause you to rest. [I will ease and relieve and refresh your souls.]
>
> Matthew 11:28 (AMPC)

This is an exchange. He's saying, "Give Me *that*, so I can give you *this*." If we don't give Him our weariness and burdens, we don't have room for His rest within us.

The Bible talks about *expecting* faith. Look at Abraham, who was old and had a barren wife, yet God told him he would have a child. At the word of the Lord, Abraham *expected* it, despite the physical impossibility. He didn't just hope it would happen or think it might happen—he was confident and unwavering that since God said it, it was as good as done. Anchored in faith, he refused to be passive toward the promise of God.

He staggered not at the promise of God through unbelief; but was strong in faith, giving glory to God; and being fully persuaded that, what he had promised, he was able also to perform.

Romans 4:20-21

He knew his God was faithful and honest, and he trusted that promise to come to pass for 25 years, at which time he and his wife miraculously had the child God promised them. That might sound like a long time, but if Abraham could sustain faith expectation for 25 years, that should encourage the rest of us to stay in faith expectation for the mere days, weeks, or months it takes to receive many of our petitions to the Lord—and even the petitions that take several years!

There's a difference between faith expectation and striving expectation. It's possible to start out in faith expectation but slip into striving expectation. We've probably all known people who say they're believing God for something, but time goes by, and before you know it, their words reveal that they're not in faith expectation anymore. There's a noticeable difference between the two. Faith has a certain sound, posture, and presence.

Faith expectation speaks the Word of God, prays to God and praises Him for the victory, and doesn't stop. One of my pastors has talked about the reality of some people getting to Heaven, seeing the Lord, and asking Him why He didn't do through them what they felt He would do, and the Lord's response is they kept giving up right before their breakthrough. We don't want that to be our story; we want to go the distance and cross the finish line. It's always darkest before the dawn, but the Lord is with you, and He will *never* fail you. You can trust Him completely. He is worthy of our continual faith expectation. As a faithful God, He requires us to be a faithful (full of faith) people.

> But without faith it is impossible to please Him, for he who comes to God must believe that He is, and that He is a rewarder of those who diligently seek Him.
>
> Hebrews 11:6 (NKJV)

Striving expectation is different. It's uncertain and unstable. There's an ellipsis where there was once an exclamation point, and there's heaviness instead of joy. While faith expectation has an energetic, life-giving atmosphere, striving expectation has a fatigued, draining, or pressured atmosphere. It's unmistakable.

We can imagine why there's a stark contrast here. Look at your strength and ability; think about what you're capable of. Can you craft a universe with a breath? Does sickness and disease bow to your name? Yet, the strength and ability of the Alpha and the Omega, Almighty God, the Author and Finisher of your faith...He accomplishes all of that and so much more. What an incomparable contrast: our strength and His!

> Therefore we also, since we are surrounded by so great a cloud of witnesses, let us lay aside every weight, and the sin which so easily ensnares us, and let us run with

endurance the race that is set before us, looking unto Jesus, the author and finisher of our faith, who for the joy that was set before Him endured the cross, despising the shame, and has sat down at the right hand of the throne of God.

Hebrews 12:1-2 (NKJV)

This race we're running, we're running it at our own pace. Our specific assignments differ, and the dreams and talents the Lord has placed within us are unique. We are not the same. Comparison and jealousy have no place among us.

The delays you think you're experiencing do not have to be your disqualification—they are certainly not God disqualifying you. He does not want to thrust you into places you're crying out for just to have you fall flat on your face because you were unprepared. He's a good Father. He cares more about you than *you* care about you! His heart is filled with more love for you than you can imagine. If we're trapped in condemnation, taking on blame and shame for not being where we think we're supposed to be, we can't receive His peace that says we're on our way and He will help us get there. A process of preparation is not a punishment—it's protection.

But in a great house there are not only vessels of gold and of silver, but also of wood and of earth; and some to honour, and some to dishonour. If a man therefore purge himself from these, he shall be a vessel unto honour,

sanctified, and meet for the master's use, and prepared
unto every good work.

2 Timothy 2:20-21

When you undergo proper preparation, God says you
are a vessel of honor, sanctified, and both useful and
profitable to Him. He says there are vessels of dishonor,
but as we submit to His Word and His timing, we are
vessels of honor.

Do not despise these small beginnings, for the Lord
rejoices to see the work begin.

Zechariah 4:10a (NLT)

We must trust Him! We see small beginnings,
sometimes so small that we may wonder if we are truly
beginning, but it's vital to see what God sees. He *rejoices* to
see the work begin! Yes, He loves to accelerate us and
establish us, but first we must *begin*. Instead of letting
questions, doubts, or unbelief circle in our thoughts and
plant seeds in our heart, we must trust Him and rejoice. If
He's rejoicing, what ought we be doing?

God cares more about who you're becoming than how
fast you arrive. This life is a vapor, but He's waiting for
you to be ready for where He's taking you. He's not
pushing you out the door like earthly parents sometimes
do these days when their child turns 18 years old, often
without properly preparing them for what they must do
and how they must handle things. God is not like that.

This is not to say He will not accelerate you in your process. He absolutely will! When you are pressing through whatever comes, abiding in Him and applying His instructions and corrections, you are going to get where you are going faster than you would otherwise. He multiplies your efforts when you are obedient to and led by Him.

But let him ask in faith, nothing wavering. For he that wavereth is like a wave of the sea driven with the wind and tossed. For let not that man think that he shall receive any thing of the Lord. A double minded man is unstable in all his ways.

James 1:6-8

And I, brethren, could not speak unto you as unto spiritual, but as unto carnal, even as unto babes in Christ. I have fed you with milk, and not with meat: for hitherto ye were not able to bear it, neither yet now are ye able. For ye are yet carnal: for whereas there is among you envying, and strife, and divisions, are ye not carnal, and walk as men?

1 Corinthians 3:1-3

Blessed is the man that walketh not in the counsel of the ungodly, nor standeth in the way of sinners, nor sitteth in the seat of the scornful.

Psalm 1:1

You will make significantly greater progress if you are staying in faith, growing in the Lord, and keeping godly associations.

About four months into being married to my husband, I visited my parents out of state and spent a week attending revival meetings morning and night with them. I experienced more of God's presence and power in those eight days than I had in all the prior years of my life combined. It's no wonder I wanted to pack up, move, and go to Bible school there.

As much as I trusted what God could and would do in my life if I did all that, I knew I had a husband back home that didn't attend any of the services with me. We didn't even go to church or pray. We'd had many conversations about growing up in church, but between the two of us, we had seen hypocrisy, heard wrong doctrine, and experienced ungodly church leadership. We had only been married a few months, and all I could think was the urgency I felt in my heart would rip the rug out from under my husband. That trip was in January, and I knew I felt the Lord calling me to start school in August.

Because I didn't trust the Lord with the timeline or my marriage, it was a tumultuous several months. But it was *God's* timeline. Even though I made mistake after mistake, I also cried out to the Lord privately more than I had ever done in my life, determined to grow in the things of God, learned about the creative power and authority in my words, and sought counsel and agreement from believers much stronger in faith than I was at the time. As a result, the Lord stayed with me and worked with me, I drew a line in the sand and declared the devil could not have my marriage, and my husband moved to join me a few days before the school year started. It was a total miracle. Bless God, we are happily married today and continuing to step into more of the Lord's call on our lives.

When you're working with God's timeline, you can trust Him and have zero questions or worries. He doesn't make mistakes or change His mind.

But if you're locked in to *your* timeline, you must surrender it to Him. He doesn't fit into our plans. He is much bigger than our plans, and He knows infinitely more than we do. We must surrender our expectations to Him if they don't come from Him. He's not breathing on our efforts just because we love Him and desire Him. He's breathing on our efforts because we're obedient to Him and honoring Him.

> My soul, wait thou only upon God; for my expectation is from him.
>
> Psalm 62:5

Sometimes, you need to tell your soul what to do. Your mind, will, and emotions make up your soul. David instructed his soul multiple times in his psalms to the Lord, because he understood that while his soul might not want to obey God or make the effort to seek Him, it was disobedience and dishonor toward God to do any less. We ought to instruct our soul, as David did:

> Bless the Lord, O my soul; and all that is within me, bless His holy name! Bless the Lord, O my soul, and forget not

all His benefits: Who forgives all your iniquities, Who heals all your diseases, Who redeems your life from destruction, Who crowns you with lovingkindness and tender mercies, Who satisfies your mouth with good things, so that your youth is renewed like the eagle's.

Psalm 103:1-5 (NKJV)

David questioned his soul as well. He openly acknowledged his soul and its attitude, not trying to hide anything from the Lord, but instead commanding his soul to rise up from a miserable place and hope in God.

Why are you cast down, O my soul? And why are you disquieted within me? Hope in God, for I shall yet praise Him for the help of His countenance.

Psalm 42:5 (NKJV)

Any time the pressure of time tries to set itself on our shoulders, we give it to the Lord. This is the divine exchange: we give that pressure to Him, and He gives us His peace. We don't get distracted or burdened with worry, anxiety, or despair. This is the covenant we have with Him and the promise we have from Him. We trust Him. We trust Him completely, with everything.

Today, you can give up clinging so tightly to your version of the future and instead receive the one God has prepared. Today's your day for freedom from the bondage of "behind" and entrance into the "becoming" that God sees. You can walk with purpose without getting burdened with pressure. Stay close to your Heavenly Father. He is with you, and He doesn't fail.

**Declare this Word
over yourself and your life today:**

The Lord is my shepherd; I shall not want. He maketh me to lie down in green pastures: he leadeth me beside the still waters. He restoreth my soul: he leadeth me in the paths of righteousness for his name's sake. Yea, though I walk through the valley of the shadow of death, I will fear no evil: for thou art with me; thy rod and thy staff they comfort me. Thou preparest a table before me in the presence of mine enemies: thou anointest my head with oil; my cup runneth over. Surely goodness and mercy shall follow me all the days of my life: and I will dwell in the house of the Lord for ever.

Psalm 23

CHAPTER NINE

Give Up the Struggle Bus

FROM STRIVING TO STRENGTH

Maybe your seat on the struggle bus isn't as sunken in as mine was. Maybe it's *more* sunken in. Either way, the moment you stand up, see it for what it is, and know there's a better way, you can walk right off that bus and be done with it.

The moment you stand up is the moment you realize what you're doing isn't working.

The moment you see that sunken seat for what it is, is the moment you know *exactly* which areas of your life that striving has become normal.

The moment you know there's a better way is the moment you recognize surrender as the solution.

The moment you walk off that bus is the moment you lay everything down before the Lord, accepting His divine exchange: your ability for His ability, your weakness for His strength, your plans for His plans.

Until you have a revelation of this, that struggle bus might look an awful lot like endurance, commitment, diligence, faithfulness, wisdom, or maturity. But if you know you're pushing or pressured, and it's draining and unsustainable, it's not God wearing you down.

My grace is sufficient for thee: for my strength is made perfect in weakness.

2 Corinthians 12:9a

But thanks be to God, Who in Christ always leads us in triumph [as trophies of Christ's victory] and through us spreads and makes evident the fragrance of the knowledge of God everywhere,

2 Corinthians 2:14 (AMPC)

He lifts you up, and He gives you His grace to do what you can't do on your own. Striving pushes away His grace, even if you desire His grace.

No deception can stand its ground in the presence of God. This is why your life of peace and freedom only comes from your relationship with Him. He is the source, not us or our supposed success. He restores, revives, refreshes.

Whosoever drinketh of the water that I shall give him shall never thirst; but the water that I shall give him shall be in him a well of water springing up into everlasting life.

John 4:14

He's everything, and He never fails or leaves us. He wants you to release what He's delivered you from, not struggle with it.

Starting out in faith will end up in force if we're trying to do it ourselves. When we take our eyes off Jesus and fix them on the task or situation, it's like we're tying God's hands and pushing Him back. We must stay with Him and keep our focus on Him. That's how we stay in His peace and out of pressure, with trust in Him and not tension within, in obedience rather than overwhelm.

The continual posture of our heart must be, "Lord, I need You. I needed You then, I need You now, and I need You up ahead." It's not, "I've got this," it's, "Lord, thank You that *You've* got this." When He's our everything, we never lack, run dry, wear out, or fall apart.

If we don't keep that heart posture, if He's not *everything* to us, we might not intend to or want to, but we find ourselves taking this burden and that pressure, this frustration and that stress. It's all too easy to slip into striving.

I beseech you therefore, brethren, by the mercies of God, that ye present your bodies a living sacrifice, holy, acceptable unto God, which is your reasonable service. And be not conformed to this world: but be ye transformed by the renewing of your mind, that ye may prove what is that good, and acceptable, and perfect, will of God.

Romans 12:1-2

One of my favorite pastors says, "The problem with a living sacrifice is that it's always trying to crawl off the altar." We're the living sacrifice. On the altar, we're surrendered fully. Crawling off the altar, we're taking on burdens and bondages that God delivered us from. We must stay surrendered. We must stay on the altar—living with Him, flowing from Him, and abiding in Him.

Have you ever equated pressure with progress? I once had the idea that the harder I worked, the more I accomplished, and the more I accomplished, the more I was growing and leveling up. Hard work, as in diligence, is important and godly. Hard work, as in striving, is ultimately being distracted from divine instruction and guidance. So, if diligence is the heart behind hard work, it's productive, and greater grace comes to match what's needed for the work to be done. However, if striving is the heart behind hard work, it's taxing, and the work gets harder to do.

The number one thing that stops someone from getting off the struggle bus is fear. They think thoughts such as:

What happens if I stop pushing myself so hard?

What if I let this person down?

What if scaling back to what I really have capacity for makes me look weak because I'm doing less or not seen as much?

If I take time to rest, am I just being lazy or disobedient?

This person may lose faith in me if I don't keep the pedal to the metal.

All of those thoughts are fear-based. Can you hear it? It's the fear of the unknown, fear of others' opinions, fear of losing someone's approval, or fear of not being faithful.

We can't allow fear to dictate our decisions. Fear is a device of the devil to hold us back from what God has for us.

> Leave no [such] room or foothold for the devil [give no opportunity to him].
>
> Ephesians 4:27 (AMPC)

> For God hath not given us the spirit of fear; but of power, and of love, and of a sound mind.
>
> 2 Timothy 1:7

Do you desire to hear from the Lord, clearly and specifically? I know I do! Striving muffles clarity, the same way a weak radio station comes through with a lot of static and sometimes cuts out altogether. We don't want to miss the Lord's voice; we want to hear Him crisp and clear, right away, and know with confidence we're hearing from Him.

Do you recall a time you overloaded your schedule? If you were to seek out advice from a godly leader, spiraling in burnout, there's a good chance they would tell you to pray about where you need to make some changes. Some people in that position might think, *I can't hear the Lord right now...that's how tired I am!* In the state they're in, it's probably true; they can't hear God at all because they aren't tuned in to Him. We can try to do many things for Him, but we're unable to hear His voice when we're tuned in to something else. If we're ever in that place, we must run to Him, repent, and receive His forgiveness and love. Once our relationship is in focus again, we can hear His voice and receive His direction.

Spiritual discernment sharpens and comes into clearer focus as we release striving and keep ourselves from drifting back into it. That means we pick up on the checks we feel in our spirit when something is off, as well as the peace that comes in our spirit when things are right.

> And the Lord said, My Presence shall go with you, and I will give you rest.
>
> Exodus 33:14 (AMPC)

It's the Lord's plan for His presence to be with us everywhere we go, all the time. He's already chosen us, but we must choose Him. He's given us freewill, and He can't take it back because He is just and doesn't lie. We can take every step with His presence, and as we do, He gives us rest. There's no internal striving weighing us down and no external obstacle stopping us.

Clarity and discernment aren't the only things we miss out on in striving mode. We also decrease or deplete our capacity to receive and operate in joy, and to relate to and respect other people. God's signature creation is people, so if we're about His business, other people are involved. To represent Him well, we must have joy and manage relationships respectfully.

If you can pinpoint a time when you've been full-on striving, do you realize how small your perspective became in that mode? Yet, in the anointing, in the presence of God, big dreams and big visions are practically explosive, bursting forth on the inside of you. That's because on our own, we're limited to this temporal realm, this earthly life, this moment, these struggles, and these obstacles. But with the mind of God, divine purpose floods our whole being, visions are realized that are far beyond our ability alone, and the gift of faith can flow freely to give us an anchor to withstand the winds and the waves. We can hear the word of the Lord, adding strength to our anchor. His voice is clear, and we invite Him into every detail. Everything is so much easier if we'll just stay with Him!

Someone might be thinking, *That's great. I wish I'd understood this a while ago and done some things differently.* You're in good company, because me too! We can't do anything about the past, but we can absolutely do better going forward. And remember, God promises to redeem the time the enemy has stolen:

> And I will restore or replace for you the years that the locust has eaten—the hopping locust, the stripping locust, and the crawling locust, My great army which I sent among you.
>
> Joel 2:25 (AMPC)

Ask Him to give you a greater revelation and awareness of His love for you, that He would even redeem lost time in your life. Oh, how He loves us!

Would you like to know the true key to being faithful?

You will guard him and keep him in perfect and constant peace whose mind [both its inclination and its character] is stayed on You, because he commits himself to You, leans on You, and hopes confidently in You.

Isaiah 26:3 (AMPC)

Trust in him at all times; ye people, pour out your heart before him: God is a refuge for us. Selah.

Psalm 62:8

Remain in His rest. We're not here to lounge around or coast; that would be laziness, not God's rest. Remaining in His rest means we trust Him, keep our confidence in Him, and hold fast to Him. Because we rest in Him, we can go farther and move faster. Old hindrances can't touch us, and old habits can't hold us. We're free in Him.

In [this] freedom Christ has made us free [and completely liberated us]; stand fast then, and do not be hampered and held ensnared and submit again to a yoke of slavery [which you have once put off].

Galatians 5:1 (AMPC)

What does it look like for you to get off the struggle bus today? What changes do you make? How do your priorities shift? Where do you find yourself breathing easier and accessing more joy?

It's *always* a good day to get off the struggle bus.

Pray this prayer:

Father, thank You that whom the Son sets free is free indeed. I declare on the authority of Your Word that I am free from striving, bondage, condemnation, and discouragement.

As Your Word declares, I am the righteousness of God in Christ Jesus, You are my source and supply, and no weapon formed against me shall prosper. I choose to live the high life that You have called me to, and my life shall be a testimony of Your goodness for Your glory.

I am not subject to or ignorant of the devil's devices, for I abide in the secret place of the Most High. I am well able to overcome whatever comes my way, because greater are You in me than he that is in this world.

Thank You, Lord, for an unshakable faith within me and this victorious life I'm living in Your strength according to Your plan. I love You, Lord. Thank You for Your perfect love working in me and working through me to bless Your precious people. Great is Your faithfulness!

In Jesus' Name, I pray. Amen.

CHAPTER TEN

Living from God's Strength

THE DIVINE EXCHANGE

WHEN STRIVING HAS LEFT THE BUILDING, WHAT ARE WE left with? If we are not doing that anymore, what are we doing instead?

In Numbers 13, the Lord tells Moses to send spies into Canaan, the land that He had promised to His people. Moses selected the spies and sent them out with this instruction:

> And see the land, what it is, and the people that dwelleth therein, whether they be strong or weak, few or many; and what the land is that they dwell in, whether it be good or bad; and what cities they be that they dwell in, whether in tents, or in strong holds; and what the land is, whether it be fat or lean, whether there be wood therein, or not. And be ye of good courage, and bring of the fruit of the land. Now the time was the time of the firstripe grapes.

> Numbers 13:18-20

So the spies searched out the land and gathered their impression. When they returned to Moses, this is what they said:

And they told him, and said, We came unto the land whither thou sentest us, and surely it floweth with milk and honey; and this is the fruit of it. Nevertheless the people be strong that dwell in the land, and the cities are walled, and very great: and moreover we saw the children of Anak there. The Amalekites dwell in the land of the south: and the Hittites, and the Jebusites, and the Amorites, dwell in the mountains: and the Canaanites dwell by the sea, and by the coast of Jordan.

And Caleb stilled the people before Moses, and said, Let us go up at once, and possess it; for we are well able to overcome it.

But the men that went up with him said, We be not able to go up against the people; for they are stronger than we. And they brought up an evil report of the land which they had searched unto the children of Israel, saying, The land, through which we have gone to search it, is a land that eateth up the inhabitants thereof; and all the people that we saw in it are men of a great stature. And there we saw the giants, the sons of Anak, which come of the giants: and we were in our own sight as grasshoppers, and so we were in their sight.

Numbers 13:27-33

What a mess! But this is exactly what happens with us today when we are looking at our ability and considering our limitations. If you keep reading in Numbers 14, you see the whole of Israel in an uproar against their God-ordained leaders and even the plan of God. Caleb and Joshua, the two spies who had gone in and believed the report of the Lord, that the land was theirs to take, compelled Israel to trust in God rather than rebel against Him, and to not fear the people in the land.

However, the Israelites weren't commanding their soul to bless and trust God like David would years later in his psalms. The Lord had done mighty miracles time and time again, but the people were stubborn, untrusting, and complaining. They wanted to strive in their own strength, as they'd done for generations of slavery in Egypt.

Whatever the Lord delivers us from, we must be delivered all the way—spirit, soul, and body. To walk in His freedom and live in His rest, we must disassociate from the bondage that once held us. We are a free people, and we must have soft hearts.

> I will give you a new heart and put a new spirit within you; I will take the heart of stone out of your flesh and give you a heart of flesh.
>
> Ezekiel 36:26 (NKJV)

The new heart the Lord gives us is soft and receptive to Him, His presence, and His plan. The ten spies that "brought up an evil report" didn't have soft hearts that relied on God; they had hard hearts that saw their own inadequacy and inability, much like this depiction:

Yea, they made their hearts as an adamant stone,

Zechariah 7:12a

We're not striving like the majority of the Israelites were at that time. Today, striving has left the building. We're living from God's strength. We're remaining in His rest. His peace, provision, and protection are our portion. In our rising up and our lying down, He sustains us and carries us.

Our tense muscles relax, and our smiles come easier. Our focus is present but not pressured. Our thoughts are relevant and responsive, rather than racing or reactive. Our prayers have fresh purpose and power, because our relationship with God is close, connected, and candid. What is that?

Friend, that's *surrender*. We have laid everything down that has held us back, and we are finally free to move forward in the right direction at a healthy and faithful pace. We are not just observers or followers of Jesus—we are an extension of Him.

Just about all of us have experienced burnout before. That's a result of striving and mismanagement. At the breaking point of burnout, all that seems possible is rest. But that rest is a physical, mental, or emotional reset, at best. What we need is a *spiritual* reset, deliverance to not only recover from the burnout but resist returning to the place that caused it in the first place.

Fear not, for I am with you; be not dismayed, for I am

your God. I will strengthen you, yes, I will help you, I will uphold you with My righteous right hand.

Isaiah 41:10 (NKJV)

Lean on, trust in, and be confident in the Lord with all your heart and mind and do not rely on your own insight or understanding. In all your ways know, recognize, and acknowledge Him, and He will direct and make straight and plain your paths.

Proverbs 3:5-6 (AMPC)

Be careful for nothing; but in every thing by prayer and supplication with thanksgiving let your requests be made known unto God. And the peace of God, which passeth all understanding, shall keep your hearts and minds through Christ Jesus.

Philippians 4:6-7

Offering our true obedience to the Lord means the entirety of our dependence is on Him. We're not carrying the what, the how, the where, the who, or the when. He carries all of that, guiding our steps so we can walk it out His way.

This doesn't mean we're mindless robots. My relationship with God is not the same as your relationship with God. We don't all speak to Him the same way, and He doesn't speak to each of us the same way. We each have our own relationship with our Heavenly Father, just as children each have their own unique relationship with their earthly parents. He made us unique with our own personality, communication style, quirks, humor, and preferences. He didn't make us all the same, and we won't do things quite the same as each other, for the most part.

Think of the worship team at your church. Two drummers are different from each other. One guitarist is distinct from another. Two soprano singers lead the same song, and the song varies between their leading styles. An alto singer leads the same song and takes yet another approach. The voices, vocal cues, and physical expressions are likely far from identical.

Similarly, four people working together on the same creative assignment are going to bring their own unique flares to it, with different approaches and a collaborative exchange of ideas as the project begins to take shape. They're not all thinking the same thoughts and finishing each other's sentences. They have their own ideas to share with the group, and one person's idea can spark an idea from someone else.

Some of us enjoy "people watching" at times, because people can be so very interesting, and even downright inspiring, as we watch them in their element. We are all different, and when we're embracing those differences in ourselves and each other, we gain the benefits the Lord intended from our combined efforts.

This is how God made us. This is how He sees us. Our surrender to Him is not emptying us of originality—He created that originality! Rather, our surrender to Him frees us to be the best version of *us* because our load is lightened by *Him* and our path is lit up by *Him*.

Continually surrendering our everything to Him is basically our "freedom maintenance." We get to keep walking in His freedom. It's that divine exchange we've talked about. "Lord, here's everything that I'm feeling tired, weighed down, and burdened from. I'm here for Your rest. I'm here for Your peace. I'm here for Your joy. I'm here for Your vision, which is infinitely greater than mine could ever be. Lord, I love You! Thank You for always loving me and never forsaking me. I want every moment to be in Your presence, because that refreshing infuses me with Your strength. I cannot thank You enough, Lord."

> Humble yourselves therefore under the mighty hand of God, that he may exalt you in due time: casting all your care upon him; for he careth for you.
>
> 1 Peter 5:6-7

When striving tries to creep back in, when that pressure comes knocking or that burden tries to rest on your shoulders again, close your eyes, lift your hands, and initiate the divine exchange again. This is a fresh consecration to the Lord, rejecting the notion to strive and receiving the precise and promised provision you need from the Lord in that moment.

> Draw near to God and He will draw near to you.
>
> James 4:8a (NKJV)

God's strength will carry you everywhere, all the days of your life, beyond anything you could have thought possible or imagined doing. It's your hands, your feet, and your mouth being inspired by His blueprints and His vision. His plan for you is unique to you; it's the purpose He placed on the inside of you before you were ever born. Stepping into that divinely ordained plan is the most liberating, unstoppable, victorious place you'll ever find yourself on this Earth. Allowing Him to restore your joy means you're inviting His strength, and His peace becomes your standard mode of operation.

> For this day is holy to our Lord. Do not sorrow, for the joy of the Lord is your strength.
>
> Nehemiah 8:10b (NKJV)

> And let the peace (soul harmony which comes) from Christ rule (act as umpire continually) in your hearts [deciding and settling with finality all questions that arise in your minds, in that peaceful state] to which as [members of Christ's] one body you were also called [to live]. And be thankful (appreciative), [giving praise to God always].
>
> Colossians 3:15 (AMPC)

If faith is the stairway to victory, praise is the escalator! When you praise God, you're saying you have faith in Him and His promises, and you have set your sight on the victory so boldly, that you can't help but thank Him and see Him for the faithful God and good Father that He is. Declare the Word of the Lord. Declare unshakable strength. Declare victory and refuse defeat. Remember He who is in you, He who goes before you, the Defender behind you. Infuse your walk of faith with praise, and you will live from more of God's strength.

One of my pastors has shared stories about couples on the verge of a divorce. In the presence of God, those couples were touched by God, and when they came back together, all the issues were sorted out. Although we've never been on the verge of divorce, my husband and I have experienced serious healing in our own marriage in the presence of God. Why is that? Because anything that binds you or weighs you down must *bow* to the Almighty. God wants to restore marriages. When both desire to have what God wants, they each make room for the deep work that needs to be done in their own heart.

He heals the brokenhearted and binds up their wounds [curing their pains and their sorrows].

Psalm 147:3 (AMPC)

There is no pain He can't remove, no sting He can't take out, and no heartbreak He can't heal. He's in the business of making you whole, nothing lacking, ever.

Beloved, I wish above all things that thou mayest prosper and be in health, even as thy soul prospereth.

3 John 2

Think about this for a few minutes, genuinely and without distraction: What are the *dreams* inside of you? If money were no object, if time was no binding factor, if where you live or what job you're working didn't have a say in where you're headed … *What are the dreams inside of you?* What's been with you longer than you can remember? What's in there, deep within you? What have you pictured yourself doing? Where can you picture yourself going?

Smile. Let His joy bubble up from within you. If it starts as a chuckle, let it out. If it comes forth as a great belly laugh, let it out. His joy is your strength—it's His strength infusing your whole being to accomplish that which He's placed on the inside of you.

> Let them shout for joy, and be glad, that favour my righteous cause: yea, let them say continually, Let the Lord be magnified, which hath pleasure in the prosperity of his servant.
>
> Psalm 35:27

> Delight yourself also in the Lord, and He will give you the desires and secret petitions of your heart.
>
> Psalm 37:4 (AMPC)

The Lord delights in your prosperity, and He gives you the desires of your heart. How do you know for sure that He gives you the desires of your heart? Because your heart is toward Him and you're moving with the mind of God, not temporal or selfish desires.

Don't listen to the "buts" and the "what ifs"—they have no business in your dreams except to extinguish them.

Come alive to the big things the Lord has placed within you. Let Him infuse you with His strength.

Dare to dream the dreams within you and step into them God's way, *in His strength*.

Conclusion

STAYING FREE

We have walked through the concepts of surrender, release, and exchange, and we've established there is freedom wholly granted to us through God's liberty. What does it actually feel like in your body, your mind, and your spirit now?

We are not searching our emotions for a shallow, brief moment; we're searching the deepest parts of ourselves, our core, for a true breakthrough. This is running a "systems check" to confirm we are not just diagnosing problems but resolving them.

If this book has taught you anything, it's probably how sneaky, deceptive, and manipulative striving can actually start. It's unlikely any of us read and hear the Word of God with a heart posture of love and thankfulness toward Him and blatantly think, *Well, He has great plans, that's great, but I think I've got better ones! He's going to carry my heavy burdens? No, no, no—I'm not weak, I've got it.*

Remember, in the Garden of Eden, the serpent didn't come out swinging when he approached Eve (Genesis 3:1–

5). He planted a seed of doubt: "Has God indeed said?" and he let Eve respond with what God said. Then, he inserted the lie: "No, no, that's not true. God only said that because He doesn't want you to have your eyes opened like His." The serpent was telling her God was manipulating them, but God was *protecting* them because He *loved* them.

The same is true today: He protects us because He loves us. This is why we're safest and most free when we're with Him.

In verse 6, we see where Eve *considered* the lie and decided to believe it, forsaking God's protection for the serpent's deception. She didn't instantly drop dead or feel sick to her stomach, so she decided there was no harm in what she'd done. She then invited her husband to join her in deception and disobedience, thinking it was wisdom.

Isn't that sneaky! The devil is a trickster.

> Be sober, be vigilant; because your adversary the devil, as a roaring lion, walketh about, seeking whom he may devour: whom resist stedfast in the faith,
>
> 1 Peter 5:8-9a

Our only way to stay free from his lies and tricks is to stay under the protection and direction of God.

Once your eyes are opened to these things, you grow in this revelation, and you grow in discernment. You don't fall for sneaky deceptions or trip over rocks, veering off the path God has for you. You see clearly and more clearly, and you walk out this instruction from the Lord:

Leave no [such] room or foothold for the devil [give no opportunity to him].

Ephesians 4:27 (AMPC)

Our freedom isn't up for discussion or negotiation, because it comes from God Himself, the Creator of Heaven and Earth.

Therefore if the Son makes you free, you shall be free indeed.

John 8:36 (NKJV)

In [this] freedom Christ has made us free [and completely liberated us]; stand fast then, and do not be hampered and held ensnared and submit again to a yoke of slavery [which you have once put off].

Galatians 5:1 (AMPC)

When we know where our freedom comes from, we don't question whether we have it or whether we can keep it. God is not a man that He should lie.

God is not a man, that He should lie, nor a son of man, that He should repent. Has He said, and will He not do? Or has He spoken, and will He not make it good?

Numbers 23:19 (NKJV)

Realize that Eve didn't consciously choose bondage. She thought she was choosing wisdom and becoming more like God. She was tricked, deceived. That's how striving usually tries to wedge its way into your heart and life. There's an element of diligence to guard our heart and not allow outside circumstances to overtake or overwhelm us. Our primary protection, however, is staying in close relationship with our Heavenly Father, which involves our inward posture and daily decision to belong to Him, be like Him, and obey Him.

Here are some questions you can ask yourself to identify striving in your life:

1. Is this correction from the Lord, or condemnation from the devil?
2. Is this peace from the Lord, or passivity in me?
3. Is this momentum a result of a diligent and excellent spirit, or a heavy pressure I'm holding up?
4. Is this godly wisdom, or my own inclination?
5. Is this surrender to God, or succumbing to pressure?
6. Are my eyes on Jesus, or this situation?
7. Is my heart persistently pressing in to God, or troubled and wavering in my situation?
8. Am I performing, or flowing from God's presence?
9. Is my motive my relationship with God, or my reputation with people?
10. Am I settling for my own comfort and contentment, or operating under God's grace to

allow Him to do greater through me than I can do by myself?

Pressure to perform can't just show up and rattle you. Fear can't just sneak in and run any area of your life. When you recognize the signs, the effects, and the tricky nature, you can feel the difference within yourself, asking and identifying quickly: "Is this God's strength flowing, or my flesh trying to take over?"

This book doesn't offer a quick fix, shortcut, or spiritual cliché that seems to free you up for a while but fizzles over time. We can see the solution for what it is: an ongoing process of walking this out with the Lord, a life of holy surrender to and confident trust in Him.

We're not broken people, and we're not fragile. We can confidently silence any lie from the devil that tries to tell us otherwise, because we know our God is good and He is faithful.

This is how we *stay free*.

Once striving has given way to God's strength, we can keep it that way. We stay with Him, abiding in the shadow of the Almighty.

Have not I commanded you? Be strong, vigorous, and very courageous. Be not afraid, neither be dismayed, for the Lord your God is with you wherever you go.

Joshua 1:9 (AMPC)

Salvation

As you have been reading this book, maybe the Lord has been tugging at your heart in light of eternity. Yes, we have this life to live on the Earth, but then the Lord's plan is for Heaven to be our home in eternity, not the devil's Hell.

If you fit into any of the three categories below, I'm inviting you to pray now.

- You don't know for sure if you are on your way to Heaven.
- You haven't received Jesus into your heart as your personal Lord and Savior.
- You want to make a fresh commitment to the Lord and be confident that you are in right standing with Him.

Pray this prayer, and mean it in your heart as you speak the words out loud:

Father, I come to You in the precious Name of Your Son, Jesus. You said in Your Word, if I confess with my mouth and believe in my heart, that I will be saved. Forgive me of my sins. Wash me and cleanse me. Set me free. Jesus, I believe that You died for me, You rose from the dead, and You're coming back again for me. I forgive anyone who has ever hurt me, and I forgive myself. I'm saved, I'm born again, I'm forgiven, and I'm set free. Thank You, Lord, for saving me now. Give me a passion for the lost, a hunger for the things of God, and a holy boldness to preach the Gospel of Jesus Christ. I love You, Lord. In Jesus' Name, I pray. Amen.

As a minister of the Gospel of Jesus Christ, I tell you today that your sins are forgiven you right now. Always remember to run to God and not from Him, because He loves you and has a wonderful plan for your life.

About the Author

Elizabeth Wilson is the founder of Nova Sei Press, a publishing house committed to releasing Christian-authored books with excellence and helping self-publishing authors bring their projects to life with clarity and care. She studied at River University in Tampa, Florida, where her love for Scripture and ministry deepened.

Elizabeth lives in Tennessee with her husband and daughter. Her writing reflects her heart to encourage believers to live surrendered, rooted in truth, and confident in God's strength.

In addition to this book, Elizabeth has authored the Seeds of Significance series. These are seven-day devotionals designed to plant biblical truth in everyday life. Each book offers short, Scripture-centered readings that take about five minutes a day, making it simple to stay rooted in God's Word even in a full season of life. *Before You Give Up* is the first volume in the series, inviting readers to cultivate steady faith through small, daily surrender.

instagram.com/novaseipress
facebook.com/novaseipress
youtube.com/novaseipress

Nova Sei Press

Nova Sei Press exists to publish Christian-authored books with excellence and to support independent authors through thoughtful, professional publishing services. With a focus on integrity, craftsmanship, and faithfulness to Scripture, Nova Sei Press seeks to steward words that strengthen the Church and serve readers well.

Connect with Nova Sei Press on Instagram, Facebook, and YouTube at @novaseipress. Visit novaseipress.com for more information about upcoming releases and available editorial services, as well as to visit the online store.